Your Money

Use less – save more

Your Money

Use less – save more

An A–Z guide to making your money go further

JON CLIFT & AMANDA CUTHBERT

green books

First published in 2009 by
Green Books
Foxhole, Dartington
Totnes, Devon TQ9 6EB
www.greenbooks.co.uk

Design
Stephen Prior

Printed in the UK by Cambrian Printers, Aberystwyth.
The text paper is made from 100% recycled post-
consumer waste, and the covers from 75% recycled
material.

ISBN 978 1 900322 53 9

Contents

Introduction

Cutting down on your spending can be good news. It can give you a great opportunity to meet new people: by getting together to swap books, clothes, toys, baby gear or to buy food, you can make new friends, and helping each other feels good!

Meals from fresh ingredients made at home are often cheaper than ready-made meals, and need not take long to make; they are also tastier and more nutritious. Unlock your creative juices!

Travelling on foot or by bike, even for part of your journey, has the bonus of keeping you fit, saving on gym fees and of course saving you money – you will feel better too.

It is almost always cheaper to do things that benefit the environment: for example, a bottle of vinegar and some bicarbonate of soda can be used in place of many cleaning products and cost a fraction of the price. 'Reduce, reuse, recycle' saves cash in almost every area of life.

The less you buy, the more cash you have in your pocket and the fewer goods there are going to landfill and polluting the planet – and there's a lot of free stuff to be had, if you can take time to find it.

So use this book to have fun, be more self-sufficient and get together with others to share costs. Whether it's buying in bulk, watching a DVD with friends or organising a clothes swap party, you'll save money.

A–Z guide

AGE CONCERN

A charity for older people that can help with free money advice. The Age Concern adviser can check to see if you are claiming all your benefits, help you fill in your claim form, and might even be able to come and visit you if you have problems leaving your home.

www.ageconcern.org.uk ☎ **0800 00 99 66** to find your local branch.

ALCOHOL

Drinks, especially if you are socialising, can be a large part of your budget. If you are out for a night on the town, you can control your budget by having a kitty where everybody puts the same amount into a pot to fund the evening's drinks. Don't forget to look for 'happy hour' deals, and if you are buying alcohol for drinking at home, look for deals in local shops.

B

Have fun brewing your own beer and/or making your own wine, either using kits or using cheap or even free fruit such as windfall apples. It's great fun and very satisfying – especially if other people like it!

BABIES – see also Nappies, Toys

Baby clothes and equipment

Babies and young children change size so quickly that to buy new clothes and equipment all the time can be very expensive.

You may find a bargain in your local charity shop, or be able to swap children's clothing and equipment with other parents. It's a great way to get out and meet others, and to save loads of money. You can either organise a clothes swap session yourself – maybe by mentioning it to other parents at pre-school – or by contacting your local NCT (National Childbirth Trust). The NCT organises nearly-new sales where you can both sell your unwanted clothing as well as buy baby stuff such as prams, pushchairs, highchairs, etc.

www.nct.org.uk ☎ **0300 3300 770** to see where your nearest nearly-new sale is being held.

Be aware when buying second-hand goods that older electrical products, such at sterilisers, may no longer be working properly and that bottles, teats and similar products may be made of plastic made before January 2007 – these may contain substances that are now banned.

Baby milk and food

If you are about to have a baby and are considering whether or not to breastfeed, then don't forget that breast milk is totally free and requires no extra equipment. It really is the original, instant, ready-made meal and contains all the nutrients your baby needs for the first six months.

When you want to move your child on to solid food, don't be tempted by all the adverts for ready-made baby food. Although useful occasionally and extremely convenient, this can prove to be very expensive. You can make wonderful solid food for your baby costing almost nothing at all, but do talk to your health visitor or doctor about what type of food is suitable for babies at different ages; it is not advisable to give solid food before six months. Part or all of your own meal can often be mashed up with a fork and used to feed your baby. This is a great way to get your baby used to the tastes and textures of your family food.
www.eatwell.gov.uk/agesandstages

B

A really simple way of making plenty of tasty instant baby food is to freeze small portions in ice-cube trays. Put the frozen food cubes into a freezer bag, label them, and put them into your freezer. But do remember to heat them through thoroughly and leave to cool before giving the food to your baby. There are a few common-sense 'rules' you will need to follow to keep your baby safe and healthy; talk to your health visitor or look online.

Baby-sitting

Baby-sitting circles are the perfect way to have a night out and make friends with other parents in your area. Members of the group baby-sit for each other for free, with somebody keeping a tally of who sat and when. This normally works on a simple points system, with extra points given to those who baby-sit after midnight. All it needs is someone to start a circle – how about you? Get one started by letting other parents know; doctor's surgeries are a great place to advertise, and ask your health visitor to spread the word. Most baby-sitting circles change the organiser every couple of months to spread the workload.

BANKRUPTCY

If you think you are about to become bankrupt, or are consider-ing making yourself bankrupt, get advice as soon as possible.

For free, confidential and impartial advice go to the Citizens Advice Bureau, or consult an independent organisation such as the Bankruptcy Advisory Service, who offer impartial advice for a small fee.

www.citizensadvice.org.uk ☎ **0844 848 9600**
www.bankruptcyadvisoryservice.co.uk ☎ **01423 799141**

BANKS & OTHER FINANCIAL INSTITUTIONS

Providing you are sensible with your accounts and remember that the bank is a commercial business that will try to make money out of you, then banks can provide a good facility without costing you a penny.

Stay in credit

You will not be charged for your basic account if you stay in credit and may even make money, depending on the account.

Shop around

Shop around before deciding to use the services of a bank, e.g. for borrowing, insurance etc., as using a bank can be a very expensive option. Find the bank account that suits your specific needs.

Say no to credit cards

Credit cards can be expensive and addictive! If you have some already, then strongly consider cutting them up. Banks and other financial institutions offer us credit cards because they hope we will not pay off what we owe them at the end of the month – then they can start charging us. Check out your bank's overdraft charges – it may be cheaper to borrow money that way.

B

The only way you can make credit cards work for you is to pay off the monthly bill as soon as it arrives on your doorstep; that way you avoid charges. You can set payment up so that money from your bank account pays off your credit card bill automatically every month. Make sure you have enough money in your account to pay off this bill, as otherwise the bank will charge you heavily.

Arrange an overdraft

If you think you might have to spend more money than you have in your bank account, rather than keeping quiet about it, ask the bank for an overdraft. They may say no, but if you don't ask you don't get, and a pre-arranged overdraft is cheaper than the huge fees charged on unauthorised borrowing.

If you go into the red, even if you are overdrawn by a tiny amount, the bank can levy hefty charges daily, plus additional costs.

Stay within your agreed overdraft limit

Even if you go over your agreed overdraft limit by just a few pence, you will incur very high charges as well as additional costs.

Avoid special accounts

Unless you are sure they will actually save you money, be wary of special accounts. Your bank will not give you something for nothing; all these so-called 'privilege' or 'platinum' accounts require you to pay the bank every month in return for insurance or membership of an organisation, for example. Before considering a special account, work out whether you will be better off sticking with an ordinary account which costs nothing.

Make money on your current account

Many banks pay you interest on money you have in your current account; if yours does not, find one that does.

Talk to your bank

If you are having serious money problems, whether with a bank or a credit card company, get help. Talk to your bank or Citizens Advice Bureau – they are experienced in dealing with debt problems.

Check out your direct debits

Get a list of your monthly direct debits – do you still need them all?

www.citizensadvice.org.uk ☎ **0844 848 9600**

B

Other ways of banking

New systems of banking are emerging, for example where money can be both lent and borrowed by individuals, completely avoiding 'conventional' banks.

www.zopa.com

BARTER

A really simple method of getting goods and services without spending a penny. You swap whatever you have for whatever you want; this could be skills (gardening, dog walking, etc.) or items (rocking chairs, computer games, surfboards, etc.). There is no tax, no VAT, no cheques, no credit cards, just a delightfully simple system. In fact almost anything can be swapped; from homemade cakes to baby clothes and car rides – the opportunities are endless.

There are a number of very busy swap sites online. Check out:

www.u-exchange.com/barter-uk

www.readitswapit.co.uk a wonderful website that enables you to search for and swap books.

Local Exchange Trading Schemes

There are also a number of LETS schemes in operation, where people exchange goods or services with one another. The LETS system has been operating since 1991, and is well established.

www.letslinkuk.net to find a local group near you. If you don't have internet access, phone your council for the telephone number of your local LETS contact.

BENEFITS – see also Citizens Advice Bureau

Claim any benefits and tax credits that you are entitled to, e.g. Child Benefit, Working Tax Credit, Child Tax Credit, or cold weather payments. Your local Citizens Advice Bureau can advise you.

If you are of working age, your local job centre can give you advice on your entitlement to benefits. Some benefits can be claimed online.
www.jobcentreplus.gov.uk

If you have internet access, either at home or at your local library, spend five minutes on either of these sites to see which benefits you might be entitled to:
www.direct.gov.uk or **www.entitledto.co.uk**
www.ageconcern.org.uk ☎ **0800 00 99 66** to find your local branch: if you are an older person Age Concern can help you sort out your benefits.

BILLS – see also Citizens Advice Bureau

Take charge. If you are one of those people who does not open those brown envelopes, just in case, then this is the time to start. Find out how much you owe. Don't ignore the bills – they won't go away, and you could even end up in court or with debt collectors knocking at your door. If you simply can't see a way of paying your bills, take them to your local Citizens Advice Bureau, who offer free, independent and confidential advice. It's surprisingly helpful just talking about these problems with somebody who really knows what to do. There will nearly always be some way of managing your bills, e.g. deferred or re-scheduled payments.

Check out the cheapest way to pay – ask your supplier for the cheapest option, e.g. paying by direct debit or having bills sent by email. If you pay your bills by direct debit and are always in credit, then ask for your direct debit payments to be reduced.

BIRTHDAYS

It is important to celebrate birthdays even when times are tough – and they don't need to cost anything at all. Some of the best presents are free or cost almost nothing.

- Give your time e.g. offer to take a friend for a walk – in the park, on the beach or on the moors, or offer to baby or pet-sit.

- Give your skills – decorate a room, make a cake or some home-made wine. Or if you are good at cooking, then give the opportunity to learn how to make that lovely special curry of yours. What a great day – cook it and then eat it!

- Organise a surprise – a gathering of friends or family.

- Make your own birthday cards – they are unique.

- Give something from your garden.

B

BOOKS – see also Library

Use your library – it's free, warm in the winter, sociable, and an amazing facility. The staff can get you just about any book you want, if you don't mind waiting a little while. Your library also has DVDs, audio books, CDs and cassettes – great for long trips or if you have somebody unwell at home.

Why not read all those books on your bookshelf that you have never got round to reading? Or revisit some old favourites.

Second-hand book shops and markets are wonderful sources of cheap and plentiful books, mostly costing pence rather than pounds.
www.greenmetropolis.com for buying and selling second-hand books.

Swap your books – you can start book swapping wherever people gather regularly, from your local friendly café to your place of work.
www.readitswapit.co.uk

B

BORROWING MONEY – see Banks, Bills, Budget, Credit Rating, Debts, Loans, Savings

BREAD

If you can, shop at the end of the day for your bread – you can get real bargains: all bread, except for packaged bread, has to be sold on the day it is baked. If you have some space in your freezer, why not buy a few bags of bread rolls and freeze them.

Best of all is to bake your own bread. It really does not take long, is most enjoyable, and can become rather addictive. Loaves, rolls, pitta, nan – whatever you want you can bake. For most families, one bread-baking session over the weekend will see you through the week. You can save a considerable amount of money by buying your flour in bulk, either in a single sack or in 1.5 kg bags as part of a large order with other friends. One large tub of dried yeast will last a long time and is exceptionally good value.

BROADBAND – see also Telephone, Which?

Choosing a broadband provider is a minefield, and whatever advice is given one week may well be out of date the next. Friends and colleagues are a good bet on this occasion; ask them how much they spend, how reliable their broadband supplier is, and how long it took to set up the broadband.

B

Look out for 'free' broadband – it is almost always only available if you take another service from the same provider, and very often there are extra hidden costs involved.

Think carefully before being tied into long contracts, and always check the small print.

Free access to broadband is usually available at your local library, and at many internet cafés for the price of a cup of tea. Not quite as convenient as having it at home – but a lot cheaper.

If you are thinking of getting phone/TV/broadband in one deal, shop around for the best package; a bundled deal may not be the cheapest way of getting those services.

BUDGET – see also Debts

It is amazing how much money you can save by simply taking a look at what you are spending. Divide your expenses into essential (e.g. your council tax), and non-essential (e.g. cinema tickets) and then set about reducing the non-essential items, such as any subscriptions which you can do without, whether magazines, extra TV channels or club memberships.

Look at your expenditure in different areas and try to reduce it: for example, can you make your meals rather than buy them pre-packaged, cut down on alcohol, or use your car less?

Avoid debt by setting yourself a weekly budget and sticking to it; if possible allow for unexpected expenditure by saving a little each week or month into a separate account to cover emergencies.

If your job is insecure, start saving a little each week to provide yourself with a buffer in case the worst happens.

BUSES – see Travel

CARS

Apart from your home, your car – if you have one – is the most expensive thing you have, both to buy and to run; cars eat money, and at a tremendous rate. If you buy an average small car and do about 10,000 miles a year, it will cost you over £4,600 a year.

So the big question is – do you really need your car? How about selling it and spending a smaller amount of money on buses and trains, and the occasional taxi, and avoiding the expense of owning and running one? You will save yourself thousands of pounds every year, and there will be no expensive nasty surprises.

If you do decide that you simply can't live without your car, then there are still many ways that you can reduce your running costs: for example, by car sharing or changing your driving style.

Car sharing

If you have to use your car for regular trips, can you share it with others making a similar journey, or get a lift with other car users a couple of days a week and share the cost? Your journey may be much more pleasant and you'll cut your running costs dramatically.

www.carshare.com or **www.liftshare.com**, or phone your local council to see what schemes are operating in your area.

Driving style

The way you drive will hugely affect your fuel bill. Drive smoothly – anticipate slowing down and changing gear. A small decrease in speed will have a noticeable effect on your fuel consumption. Challenge yourself to increase your miles per gallon.

http://campaigns.direct.gov.uk
www.theaa.com/motoring_advice

Fuel

The cost of fuel varies hugely, so don't let your fuel tank get too low so that you are forced to buy expensive fuel – buy fuel when passing a garage with low prices. **www.petrolprices.com** or **www.whatgas.com** to find out where the best prices are in your area.

Maintenance

Little and often is best, and simple things – like keeping your tyres at the correct pressure and getting your car serviced at the specified mileage – reduce your petrol consumption and your running costs. Use a garage that is recommended by friends; cheap isn't necessarily best.

Purchase
Buy a car that has the minimum fuel consumption and with the lowest carbon dioxide (CO_2) emissions – the lower the emissions the less car tax you pay. Cars that emit less than 100 g/km of CO_2 will cost you nothing in car tax!
www.vcacarfueldata.org.uk
http://campaigns.direct.gov.uk to find out more.

Car insurance – see also Insurance

Taking your car temporarily off the road
If money is particularly tight at the moment then consider taking your car off the road for a while until things get easier; that way you can cash in your car tax and insurance. You will need to take it right off the road on to private land, which could be your drive. **www.taxdisc.direct.gov.uk/EvlPortalApp** gives information on Statutory Off Road Notification (SORN).

Car clubs
If you do need a car occasionally then investigate car clubs. There are many springing up all over the country, both in cities and rural areas. They are an excellent cheap way to have the use of a car when you need one. Apart from the huge financial savings they

also offer many other benefits, such as free allocated parking spaces in many towns and the ability to choose a big or small car.
www.carclubs.org.uk ☎ 0845 217 8996

CDS

Check out charity shops and market stalls to get hold of CDs at bargain prices, or borrow from your local library for a small fee. Beware of pirate copies sometimes sold through market stalls – apart from being illegal their quality will probably be very poor.

CELEBRATIONS – see Birthdays, Christmas

CHARITY SHOPS – see also Clothes

Great for clothes, linen, curtains, crockery, books, CDs and DVDs and the occasional teddy bear. Charity shops are particularly good places to find outfits for fancy dress parties.

CHRISTMAS – see also Birthdays

We all like to buy and receive gifts at Christmas but we can feel pressurised to spend loads of money on them, in addition to which some gifts are unwanted and rarely get used.

But Christmas can be inexpensive and still be fun, both for you and for your friends and family:

- Shop well ahead for presents, either in the sales or when you see a bargain, not just in the run up to the big day.

- If you are in a large family group, get together beforehand, put all your names in a hat and just buy for the person whose name you draw.

- Set a limit on the amount you will all spend on family and friends and agree it in advance.

- Very often the best presents are free; give your time – a day out walking with a friend or relative is something money just can't buy.

- Buy a live Christmas tree with roots if you can – then when the festivities are over you can plant it in your garden and reuse it next year.

- Save and reuse tree decorations and maybe add a couple of newcomers each year.

- Plan your Christmas meals so that you can use up all your leftovers, for example turkey curry on Boxing Day, with leftover Christmas pudding fried in butter.

- Can you recycle any unwanted gifts?
  www.recycleagift.com

CIGARETTES
A golden opportunity to give up!
 www.nhs.uk/smokefree

CITIZENS ADVICE BUREAU (CAB)

Your local Citizens Advice Bureau is a great place to get free, independent and confidential advice for all types of money problems, including seeing what benefits you might be entitled to and getting free legal advice about landlords and tenancies. Just talking to people with knowledge and experience can help. Get in touch with them before things get difficult.

www.citizensadvice.org.uk ☎ **0844 848 9600**

CLEANING

Cleaners of all sorts, from cream cleaners to surface cleaners and liquids to window cleaners not only cost a packet but in many cases are full of toxic chemicals. White vinegar, bicarbonate of soda, lemon juice and borax can do most of the jobs that these chemical concoctions do, and at a fraction of the price. Citric acid or lemon juice is great for removing grease and lime scale. **www.summernaturals.co.uk** ☎ **0161 338 2256** sells basic household cleaning products in bulk, including bicarbonate of soda, borax, soap nuts and white vinegar.

www.stainexpert.co.uk
www.lowimpact.org

CLOTHES

Buying new clothes can be very expensive, especially if you wear them once and then leave them unused in the back of the wardrobe.

- Buy clothes and accessories that will last and will go with the rest of your wardrobe; you'll be able to wear them again and again.

- Buying the cheapest gear is not necessarily the best value.

- Buy classic designs that will not date, things you really like.

- If you do have a big item to buy, such as a new coat, then wait until the sales; both the high street shops and online outlets offer amazing deals.

- Organize the occasional clothes swap party; they're great fun and a good excuse for a get-together.

- Borrow clothes and accessories for special occasions rather than buying something only to wear it once.

- Think simple and create your own style – it's cheaper than copying what the latest star is wearing.

- Learn to sew.

- Consider buying a sewing machine, they are not expensive – you will soon get your money back mending simple things like holes in jeans or the hem of a skirt rather than throwing the clothes away.

- Charity shops are great for bargains, especially in wealthy areas – go with a friend and have a laugh.

- Make your own original clothes using recycled material from older clothing that needs a new lease of life.

- Check out fashion swap websites.

- Buy your clothes on eBay.

www.whatsmineisyours.com
www.ebay.co.uk

COFFEE

Take a flask of tea or coffee or make drinks yourself at work rather than buying them at a coffee shop. You can easily save yourself over £1000 a year! If you love the taste of good coffee then make yourself real coffee using ground coffee beans before putting it in your flask, adding milk just before you drink it. Get yourself a stainless steel flask – it will last for ever.

> Just 2 cups of coffee every workday at £2.60 a cup sets you back about £104 a month – that's £1,248 a year.

COLD CALLING

People calling on you unannounced trying to sell you things are a nuisance and cost you money; don't get sucked into their bizarre sales talk. A polite but firm 'no thanks' before shutting the door or putting the phone down works well and is very simple – stop them before they get really started!

The Telephone Preference Service: **www.mpsonline.org.uk** ☎ **0845 703 4599** Sign up to reduce the number of cold telephone calls by registering with the TPS.

COMPETITIONS

Entering free competitions can be good fun, and surprisingly few people actually enter the many competitions in newspapers and magazines. However, be aware that entering competitions can be rather addictive. Do not pay to enter competitions and check the small print to see how you find out whether you have won – sometimes you are required to phone in on a premium rate phone number which could cost as much as the prize, but you can often simply send a postcard.

www.ukcompetitions.com
www.theprizefinder.com
www.win4now.co.uk

COMPOSTING

Home-made compost costs nothing and is great for your garden or pot plants. Use it as a mulch and cut down the amount of watering you need to do, reducing your water bill if you are on a meter. Some councils offer free compost bins.

www.gardenorganic.org.uk

COMPUTERS – see also Printers

If you are considering buying a computer for the first time, work out what it will cost you to buy and run it. Remember that on top of the purchase price comes a monthly fee to be connected to the internet, which is essential if you want to use your computer for anything other than writing letters.

Computers and their printers are surprisingly expensive, but there are always bargains to be had in the sales, or buy second-hand from a reliable source. Take somebody knowledgeable with you if you are going to buy; they could save you a lot of money. There are numerous second-hand computer websites.

You can access a computer at your local library or internet café for next to nothing and get help if you need it.

COMPUTER GAMES – see also Barter

Games can also be downloaded freely from some sites and then played online. However beware, as they will encourage you to purchase additional items.

Think twice before buying new; there are numerous second-hand games shops both in the high street and online.
www.freecycle.org for bargains.
www.u-exchange.com/barter-uk to swap games.

COOKING

There are multitude of ways to cook that save you both money and time, most of them obvious once pointed out. Organisations such as the Energy Saving Trust and probably your local council can provide tips and ideas. Why not give them a ring and see if they have a booklet available?

- Cut food into small pieces before cooking.

- Put a lid on top of the pan when you can.

- Turn down the heat once the pan has come to the boil – it will cook just as fast.

- Make one-pot meals that only need one element or gas ring, e.g. stew or risotto.

- Use only sufficient water to cover vegetables.

- Consider using a pressure cooker for some foods – it reduces cooking time and energy use.

- Use a steamer for vegetables – you can cook two or three vegetables on one element or gas ring.

- Turn off your oven 20 minutes before the end of cooking and use the residual heat.

www.energysavingtrust.org.uk ☎ **0800 512 012**

COSMETICS – see also Toiletries

Think twice before you buy expensive branded cosmetics – there are, in most cases, much cheaper unbranded products available. For example, an excellent moisturising cream will be available from your local chemist at a fraction of the price you would pay for a 'branded' product.

Why not make your own cosmetics from simple recipes that are as good, if not better, than many of the expensively advertised products containing 'miracle' ingredients.

www.starkhechara.co.uk

COUNCIL

Your local council is a great source of information and advice for money-saving ideas, such as:

- Bus routes
- Car sharing
- Cycle routes
- Energy-saving tips for your home
- Energy-saving tips for cooking
- Local Exchange Trading Schemes
- Recycling centres
- Grants available
- Library opening times.

Find the number in your local phone book or look online.

CREDIT CARDS – see Banks

CREDIT RATING

If you apply for a loan, whether a mortgage or a personal loan, the company will search your credit record; the more credit searches that are done on your credit rating, the more your credit rating goes down, so it is best to avoid too many searches if you can. A low credit rating means you may find it difficult to borrow money.

www.experian.co.uk to find out your credit rating.
www.moneymadeclear.fsa.gov.uk to learn more about credit ratings.

DEALS – see also Haggling

There are good deals to be had when the economy is not doing well, but bewarew of things that seem to be cheaper but have hidden costs. You rarely get owt for nowt!

DEBTS – see also Banks, Bills, Budget, Citizens Advice Bureau, Loans, Savings

- If you are already in debt, get help with managing it; the Citizens Advice Bureau has advisers who will give you free, confidential advice.

- Start paying off your debts rather than adding to them if you can.

- Pay off the debts which are costing you the most in interest first.

www.cccs.co.uk ☎ **0800 138 111** The Consumer Credit Counselling Service offers free debt advice – helps you analyse your debt and offers solutions.

www.moneymadeclear.fsa.gov.uk ☎ **0845 606 1234** Financial Services Authority has tips for managing your money and tackling debt.

www.adviceguide.org.uk for debt help online from the Citizens Advice Bureau, with loads of phone numbers and addresses.

www.direct.gov.uk for advice from HM Government.

DISHWASHERS

If you have a dishwasher there are several things you can do to reduce the running cost:

- Wait until it is full before using it. Don't be tempted by the 'half-load' facility, as it is nowhere near as energy efficient as washing with a full load.

- Wash pans up in the sink.

- Use the most energy-efficient programme; check out the manual – some programmes use considerably less energy and water than others. If there is a programme that avoids the 'drying phase' use it; open the dishwasher door when the wash cycle is completed to let the dishes dry.

- If you buy a new model, get an 'AAA'-rated energy-efficient model; they cost less to run and save you money in the long run.

www.energysavingtrust.org.uk ☎ **0800 512 012**

D–E

DIY – see also Repairs

Rather than throw them away, keep used screws, nails and such like in a box and reuse them whenever you can.

Similarly, save odd pieces of wood – you never know when you might need them! If you haven't got the right piece of timber, try your local recycling centre – many of them sell reclaimed timber and other materials, from baths to balustrades.

DRIVING – see Cars

DVDS – see also CDs, Computer Games

How about setting up a Home DVD group, where each of you takes it in turn to show a DVD at your house. Everybody contributes to the cost, it makes a great excuse to meet up and it costs next to nothing.

www.lovefilm.co.uk

www.swapandplay.co.uk to borrow and swap DVDs.

EATING IN

Eat in with friends; take it in turns to cook a meal – or how about everybody bringing along a different part of the meal? So much cheaper than going out and just as fun.

EATING OUT

Meet friends for lunch rather than supper, it's much cheaper. Check out any deals in your local papers.

If you want to make it cheaper still, decide before you order to have just one course – and stick to it! Alcohol adds considerably to your bill: give it a miss and you will be surprised at the difference in the cost.

If you want somebody to pay for your meal when you eat out and don't mind writing up your experience then check out **www.mysterydining.co.uk**

EBAY

A great place to find real bargains, but don't get carried away! Only look for and buy what you really need.
www.ebay.co.uk

ELECTRICAL APPLIANCES AND ELECTRONIC GADGETS – see also Electricity

Turn off everything electrical at the socket when not in use; chargers, TVs, computers, washing machines and so on all use electricity, even when in standby mode.

Use mains rather than battery-operated items. If you have to use a battery-operated appliance, use rechargeable batteries – buying new batteries each time is very expensive.

Beware of plasma screens – they use a lot more electricity than other TV screens.

In the average UK household, the TV is left on standby for more than 17 hours a day – costing you money.

To get an idea of which of your appliances is using the most electricity, and what it is costing, you can buy or hire an electricity monitor.
www.electricity-monitor.com for hiring electricity monitors by the month.

ELECTRICITY – see also Cooking, Electrical Appliances and Electronic Gadgets, Fridges and Freezers, Which?
At the risk of stating the obvious, electricity is expensive. Take control of your electricity bill – with a few simple steps you can reduce your bill considerably.

About 10% of your electricity bill goes on lighting.

- Switch off lights when not in use.

- Fit energy-efficient light bulbs – they last about 12 times longer than ordinary bulbs and consume about one fifth of the energy. They come in all shapes and sizes, including spotlights. Many energy companies and councils are even giving them away.

- Switch appliances off at the socket when they are not in use.

- If your hot water is heated by an immersion tank, turn down the water temperature; it is rather pointless heating the water so hot that you have to add cold water before you can use it. 60° C/140° F should do it.

- And if your immersion tank is not insulated, fit an insulating jacket. Otherwise about three-quarters of all the heat you have paid for is wasted. Buy one that's at least 75mm thick.

- Microwave ovens use about 80% less electricity than conventional ovens.

- Shop around for the cheapest electricity supplier. Consider using a supplier that generates electricity from non-polluting sources.

www.switchwithwhich.co.uk ☎ **01992 678 282**
www.greenelectricity.org

E

EMAIL – see also Broadband

If you have broadband at home then emails are a great way of staying in touch and cost you nothing extra once you have paid for a broadband connection, computer, etc.

But if you don't have internet access at home, pop down to your library or internet café and use their computers. Consider setting up an email address from one of the free providers such as Google, Yahoo or Hotmail so you can easily access your emails from any computer that is online.

If you have a laptop computer, take advantage of the many free WiFi spots that are now available, from cáfes to train stations. Get there and get online for free.

Beware of mobile phones with internet access as you will be charged for the time you are online if you send emails this way.

ENTERTAINMENT – see Leisure

EVENING CLASSES

They are great places to meet people, save money on your heating and learn a useful money-saving skill. Look in your local library, newsagent or paper for information.

EXERCISE

Save on membership fees – rather than paying for the gym, go running, walking or dancing, maybe making your exercise part of your daily routine.

Save on fares – try walking or cycling to work, even it it's only part of the way.

FL

FILMS – see DVDs

FLOWERS

If you have a garden you can make a lovely bouquet with your fresh-picked flowers and foliage and avoid the expense of bought flowers.

FOOD – see also Bread, Gardening, Shopping

When shopping we are frequently 'persuaded' to buy products we didn't know we wanted. Careful planning before going shopping will help you avoid temptation and can save you a lot of money.

Buying food

Plan your week's menus:

- Make a list before you go shopping – and stick to it!

- Order it online and get it delivered; many supermarkets and organic box schemes offer this service. It will save you on petrol or bus fares and will prevent you impulse-buying items you don't really need.

- Don't buy bottled water, it's really expensive – pour some tap water into a jug or bottle, cover it and put it in the fridge. You won't be able to taste the difference.

- Go shopping late in the day, especially on Saturday, and get the bargains, particularly in the supermarkets. All the fresh bread and many vegetables that are near their 'sell-by date' will be sold off more cheaply.

- Eat less meat; it's healthier for you and much cheaper. Don't be too concerned about not getting enough protein, simple meals like beans on toast provide plenty. Use lentils and other beans or pulses to bulk out your meals.

- If you do eat meat, look for the cheaper cuts and cook them slowly, e.g. scrag end of lamb, brisket of beef, belly pork, chicken drumsticks.

- Think about buying food in bulk and sharing it out amongst friends. There are large savings to be made and it turns shopping into a pleasant, sociable activity. All it needs is somebody to organise it. You?

www.suma.coop sells and delivers food in bulk.

Leftovers

Use your leftovers for another meal or cook only as much as you need. Throwing food away that you have bought is the same as throwing money into the bin.

www.lovefoodhatewaste.com

F

Shop locally

- Shop locally where you can; use your local shops, traders, market stalls, WI markets and Farmers Markets and save on petrol or bus fares.

- See if there is a local veg box scheme in your area – food is delivered for free and it need not be expensive.

Supermarkets

- Go with a list of what you want to buy. Stick to it – and don't be tempted.

- Be aware of the supermarket's tricks and strategies to try to get you to buy on impulse.

- Look out for bulk buys – check the unit prices; see for yourself whether it is good value or not. You may well be really surprised by so-called 'bargains'. Know your prices.

- Buy loose rather than packaged fruit and vegetables; that way you get the quantity you want to buy, and you can pick the ones you want.

- The same applies to 'Buy One Get One Free' (BOGOFs). Is this actually cheaper? Don't be sucked in to BOGOFs unless you can use or freeze the free one.

- If you have a choice of supermarkets, work out where the best deals are.

- Supermarket own-brand goods are normally cheaper than well-known brands – but once again check it out before you buy and don't expect things to be the same the next time you go shopping. They are after your money!

- If you have access to a computer, think about ordering online and getting goods delivered. You buy only what you want and save time and petrol money.

Grow your own

Growing your own fruit, herbs and vegetables is much easier than many people think and is possible even in a small space or in pots on a balcony. Consider replacing your lawn or front garden with vegetable beds and save money.

If your garden is not big enough to produce rows of potatoes, how about using it to grow the more expensive produce? You can save a lot of money with your own tasty fresh salads, fresh basil, globe artichokes, asparagus, etc.

If you don't have a garden or want more growing space, contact your local council to see if there are any allotments available. Allotment holders are normally a very friendly bunch of people, keen and willing to help newcomers.

www.nsalg.org.uk ☎ 01536 266576
National Society of Allotment and Leisure Gardeners

Forage

There is plenty of food for free to be found in woods and hedge-rows, but you do need to know what you are looking for and where to pick. However some fruits, such as blackberries, are easily recognisable and can provide you with lovely puddings in the autumn for free.

FREEBIES – see also Leisure

There are websites offering free products, but you will often be encouraged to purchase products or pay a considerable amount of money for postage and packing. Below are just a few – enter with your eyes wide open!

www.freebielist.com
www.free-stuff.co.uk
www.freeukstuff.com

FRIDGES AND FREEZERS

Fridges and freezers are responsible for about one third of your total electricity bill.

Your fridge and freezer are on 24 hours a day and so cost a con-siderable amount of money. But there are many things you can do to reduce their energy consumption, such as keeping them full (even with scrunched-up paper or bubble wrap), positioning them away from any heat sources (including sunlight) and not keeping the doors open any longer than necessary.

Check the door seals – if you shut the door on a five pound note and can pull the note out easily, it's time to replace the seal.

If you are replacing your fridge or freezer, check out the new 'A++' energy ratings. A++ models consume about one third of the electricity of some older types.

www.energysavingtrust.org.uk ☎ **0800 512 012** for more advice on keeping your energy bills down.

FURNITURE

If you need furniture, buy second hand or 'pre loved' items. It is much cheaper for you – you can paint the furniture or strip it to fit in with your surroundings and taste. Look in your local paper, or check out adverts in your local shops as well as local auctions; prices for ordinary furniture are remarkably low.

Many local councils run furniture recycling projects selling good quality second-hand goods at low prices. Give them a ring and see what's on offer. See if there is free furniture available through your local Freecycle group or the Furniture Re-use Network.
http://uk.freecycle.org
www.frn.org.uk ☎ **0117 954 3571** Furniture Re-use Network

G

GARAGE SALES

Garage sales are brilliant places to find bargains or even give-aways. Keep an eye on your local paper or ads in shop windows. But beware – these sales can be very addictive!

Why not have one yourself to sell all that unwanted 'stuff' that has been clogging up the attic. Make some money on a Saturday morning, enjoy yourself and reclaim that space.

GARDENING – see also Composting, Food

Growing your own food is a great way to save money and have healthy fruit and vegetables. You don't need much space to get started; many lovely plants can be grown to eat on sunny windowsills or balconies.

If you want more growing space then check out your local council to see if they have any allotments available, or put an advert in your local paper or shop window – is there someone who does not use their garden but would like some produce in exchange for letting you use their outside space?

Join the local gardening club, or if there isn't one then start one! They are great places to save money and learn from the experts. Seeds can be bought in bulk or shared using seeds saved from last year. Similarly, plants and equipment can be shared or given away. Have you got a community garden scheme in your neighbourhood? Check with your local council.

GAS – see also Cooking, Which?

If you have gas and use it for heating your home, consider the following options to reduce your gas bills:

- Turn your central heating thermostat down by 1° C.

- Set the timer so that it comes on about 30 minutes before you get up or come home in the evening. Remember to set it to switch the heating off about ½ hour before you leave in the morning or go to bed.

- Turn radiators down or off in rooms you only use occasionally.

- Insulate your loft – this is probably the simplest and most effective method of reducing your gas bill. Phone your local council to see if there is a grant available.

- If you need to get a new boiler, install a condensing boiler; they are the most efficient type and will save you money.

- Stuff scrunched-up newspaper into the chimneys of any unused fireplaces to stop heat from the room disappearing up the chimney.

- Check out the cheapest gas provider for your area.

www.which.co.uk ☎ 01992 822800 for unbiased advice.

HAGGLING

Be brave and try asking for a lower price when buying things. Whilst you probably aren't going to get the price down on a loaf of bread in your local shop, you might well find yourself being offered considerable reductions on larger items in the high street stores.

If you are enquiring about something on the phone, such as car and house insurance or broadband, ask if it is the best price they can offer. Give it a go – there is everything to gain, and you will soon increase in confidence. If you don't ask you don't get!

HAIRCUTS

- Cut your children's hair, at least until they start to notice!

- Get a trainee or your partner or friend to cut your hair.

- Have your hair cut really short and reduce the number of visits to the hairdresser.

- How about buying a beard trimmer and cutting your own hair with it – but please think about this before you start, you can't stop halfway through!

- Just grow your hair long.

H

HEALTH

Be healthy! Prevention is always better and cheaper than cure. Look after yourself: giving up smoking, taking plenty of exercise (walk to the shops or get off the bus a couple of stops earlier and walk the rest of the way) and eating healthily will all save you money in the long term.

www.nhs.uk/change4life for loads of helpful ideas and help to get you started.

Before using a prescription from your doctor, check with your pharmacist to see if there is a cheaper alternative.

HEATING – see also Gas, Electricity

If you have an open fire or a wood-burning stove, take advantage of scrap wood placed in skips – check that it is going to be thrown away and take it home for firewood. But do check that the timber has not been treated with preservatives or paint, as this can be extremely poisonous.

If you are over 60 years of age then make sure you are getting the winter fuel payment.

www.thepensionservice.gov.uk/winterfuel ☎ 08459 151515
www.homeheathelpline.org.uk ☎ 0800 33 66 99
www.citizensadvice.org.uk ☎ 0844 848 9600 for help and advice if you are struggling to pay your heating bills.

H

HELP THE AGED – see also Age Concern

Contact this charity for financial advice and to see what grants and payments you might be entitled to.

www.helptheaged.org.uk ☎ **0207 278 1114**

HIRING

Instead of buying items you might only use occasionally, consider hiring instead; almost anything can be hired, and for any length of time from an hour to a year.

Try your friends; see if you can borrow that wallpaper stripper or stepladder for the weekend.

www.erento.co.uk for a huge selection of hire companies and items available.

HOLIDAYS – see also Travel, Volunteering

Stay at home

Having a holiday does not automatically mean going abroad; why not just stay at home, turn off the computer and telephone and explore your local area. Treat yourself to days out, concerts or the cinema.

House swap

Consider a house swap, or even pet or house-sitting for a friend in another part of the country.

www.mindmyhouse.com a global house-sitting matching service.

www.geenee.com

www.homebase-hols.com house swapping site with sub-scription fee.

Get there for free

Why not work to get to your holiday destination for free or even for a small wage? Try a courier, car or yacht delivery job.

www.paragonyachting.com to find out about yacht delivery opportunities.

www.pro-driver.org ☎ **01162 777 774** for car delivery jobs if you are over 40.

Couch surf

If you don't mind sleeping on someone's sofa, couch surfing can be a great way to make friends and see the world.

www.couchsurfing.com

H

Volunteer

Check out volunteering in the UK or further afield; there are loads of opportunities – anything from working on an organic farm to going on a rainforest expedition in Costa Rica.

Cycle

For really cheap holiday travel you can't beat a bike – free maps are available from Sustrans. Use your bike in combination with trains and buses.
www.sustrans.org.uk ☎ 0845 113 0065

Walk

The UK has hundreds of walking routes – use your bus pass and why not take a tent if you have one? There is loads of information with routes and maps online.
www.walking-routes.co.uk
www.enjoyengland.com

Do a deal

If you are booking a holiday at the last minute, make an offer – they may just be glad to fill the vacancy.

Go at the last minute

Grab a bargain by booking at the last minute.
www.lastminute.com
www.expedia.co.uk for last-minute holiday bargains.

HOME HEAT HELPLINE

The Home Heat Helpline offers free advice for anyone having difficulties paying their energy bill.
www.homeheathelpline.org.uk ☎ **0800 33 66 99**

HOUSE SWAP – see Holidays

INSURANCE – see also Price Comparison Websites

Everyone tries to sell you insurance, from the bank manager to the supermarket. With any type of insurance it is vital to make sure that it covers what you want – read the small print.

When looking for insurance, it is tempting to rely on money comparison websites; however, be careful – quotes for the same insurance cover can vary, depending on which comparison site you use and the exact level of cover provided by the policy. To find the cheapest deal, you can either phone individual companies or try your local insurance broker, who will do the work for you.

It is almost always cheaper to pay insurance in one go, rather than monthly by Direct Debit. It may also be cheaper if you apply online.

The higher the excess you are prepared to pay, the cheaper the insurance.

Car

Putting your teenager on your insurance, rather than taking it out in his or her name, is usually cheapest.

Health

Do you need health insurance? Could you save some money monthly into a separate account with the best rate of interest you can find to cover health emergencies?

House contents

It costs more to have 'new for old' – would you want to buy new if your contents were damaged or stolen?

Travel

Don't automatically renew travel insurance – wait until you need it or check to see whether you are covered through your bank – some offer a fee-paying current account with free travel insurance, which can save you money, depending on the monthly fee for the account. However the cover is often minimal – be sure to check exactly what you are covered for.

INTEREST – see Loans, Mortgages, Savings

LEGAL AID – see also Citizens Advice Bureau

Hard to get these days but if you are eligible you may be lucky; your local Citizens Advice Bureau (CAB) offers initial free legal help. Some lawyers work 'pro bono' – provide free advice for selected cases. Your CAB will have details of any lawyers' firm operating 'pro bono' in your area.

Beware 'no win no fee' claims from law firms – check the small print very carefully before committing yourself.
www.adviceguide.org.uk for Citizens Law Centres.

LEISURE – see also DVDs, Evening Classes, Eating Out, Holidays, Travel, Volunteering

There are so many things you can do which don't cost any money and which often provide the opportunity to make new friends as well. Eating out, going to the pub or the coffee bar, going to the cinema or the gym all cost money – there are free alternatives! Whatever your interest, from playing the saxophone to football or gardening, why not see if there is a club locally that you could join.

Eat in

Instead of eating out, eat in! Invite friends round and each bring a dish of food to share.

Rent DVDs

Why pay for the cinema? Join a DVD rental club.
www.lovefilm.co.uk

Exercise

Rather than pay gym fees, start running, cycling or walking regularly; go for a walk in the park or on the beach.

Swim for free

If you are over 60 or under 16 some councils offer free swimming times in local pools (from April 2009). Check with your local council or swimming pool to see if there is free swimming in your area.

Play tennis

Tennis for Free is an organisation trying to increase the number of people playing tennis by working with councils to provide free courts and tuition.
www.Tennisforfree.com ☎ **0870 011 3733** to find out if there are free courts near you.

Get streetwise

Many arts festivals include free street entertainment.
www.artsfestivals.co.uk ☎ **0207 240 4532** for a list of festivals in the UK.

Free music

Some colleges offer free lunchtime concerts, or you could volunteer as a steward or for a charity at music festivals, e.g. Oxfam at Glastonbury, Leeds or Womad.

Be on the TV or radio

If you are near a radio or television recording studio, go and watch a recording of a TV or radio show.

www.bbc.co.uk/tickets for BBC TV and radio shows.

www.chortle.co.uk for free tickets to TV and radio comedy shows.

www.sroaudiences.com for free tickets to TV shows.

Be a culture vulture

Visit galleries, museums, castles, churches – many are free, e.g. London National Gallery, British Museum, the Winter Garden in Sheffield, Durham Cathedral, The Museum of Scotland in Edinburgh, the National Museum of Wales in Cardiff.

www.dofreestuff.com/england.html lists free events, museums, galleries and places to visit by county.

www.londonforfree.net lists free stuff in London.

www.nationaltrust.org.uk ☎ **0944 800 1895** for free days at some National Trust properties.

www.visitbritain.co.uk for free things to do across Britain.

LIBRARY

The library is one place where you genuinely get things for free. You can borrow books, read newspapers and magazines, go to free events and find out what is going on in your community, e.g. classes, events, activities, group meetings, and what your council is doing.

Depending on the size of your library, there may also be the opportunity to use a photocopier, send a fax, hire a meeting room or display space, book time on a computer or hire CDs and DVDs for a small fee.

LIGHTING – see Electricity

LOANS – see also Mortgages

Beware of being lured into loans with high interest rates. If you really need to borrow money, spend time researching the loan with the lowest Annual Percentage Rate (APR) and bear in mind the length of time of the loan, any early redemption penalties (not all companies charge this), and your ability to pay it back. Also check whether the quote includes Personal Protection Insurance (PPI), and therefore what the *actual* cost is. (Loans with PPI built in are more expensive, and often difficult to redeem early).

If you only need a short-term loan, consider borrowing from family if possible. If you are happy to juggle a bit, think about using a credit card with a 0% introductory rate, and transferring your balance when the period expires to another credit card with a 0% introductory rate.

Avoid loan sharks and pawn shops at all costs. Your local Citizens Advice Bureau can help you with the best way of dealing with short-term cash flow problems.

If you have a personal loan at a high interest rate, it is worth shopping around to see whether you can switch it to a cheaper provider – the money section of the weekend newspapers is a good place to start.

Make sure you have your debt in the cheapest place – for example, is it cheaper to borrow on your credit card, or on your overdraft?
www.which.co.uk for an explanation of key issues involved in personal loans.

LUNCH
Take your lunch into work, or when going out for the day or travelling a long distance; food on the go is always expensive and not always available, especially at night – a flask of tea and some favourite snacks saves a fortune.

L–M

If you have a microwave or oven at work and have leftovers from the night before that can be safely reheated, take them with you – a welcome change to sandwiches and much cheaper than buying lunch in the canteen or local shop.
www.eatwell.gov.uk

MAIL ORDER SHOPPING

You can save money by shopping by mail order, especially online – sign up to get information on deals and end-of-season offers by email. Many mail order outlets have free postage and packing at certain times, including returns. If you know what you want, and can order by phone or internet, not only do you often get a better deal but you save time, energy and travel costs.

MOBILE PHONES – see Email, Telephone

MORTGAGES

The mortgage scene is very volatile. Find a recommended mortgage broker or Independent Financial Adviser for the latest advice, and keep an eye on the money pages in the press and online.

If you are struggling to pay your mortgage, talk to your lender – can you take a payment holiday or reschedule your payments?

Consider switching your mortgage if you are outside your penalty period and you are not getting a good rate.
www.moneysavingexpert.com *or* **www.which.co.uk** for up-to-date information on rates and deals.

MUSIC – see also DVDs, Leisure
The web is a great resource for listening to music of your choice for free.
www.last.fm for a huge selection of tracks.
www.music-sites.net is an internet music community site.

NAPPIES
By using washable rather than disposable nappies you can save a lot of money and avoid sending mountains of disposables to landfill! And if you have more than one child, the savings are even greater.
Women's Environmental Network: **www.wen.org.uk**
☎ **0207 481 9004** for a cost comparison.

If you are going to use disposables, look out for special deals and consider using a cheaper nappy for daytime and a more absorbent one at night.
www.freeparentstuff.co.uk for free nappy samples.

N–P

NEWSPAPERS

If you like a daily paper, a subscription is the cheapest way of paying for it. Or of course if you have broadband you can read online versions for free, or you can visit your local library.

Students can get really cheap deals – look online.

PAPER

You can save money on paper by:

- Using email where possible.
- Using both sides of the sheet of paper.
- Recycling unwanted incoming mail by using it for notepads or for printing things that aren't important.
- Reusing old envelopes for lists and notes.
- Buying printer paper by the box rather than the ream – or get together with friends to buy larger amounts.
- Looking out for cheap deals in stationers and supermarkets.
- Making your own greetings cards – cheap and fun and a great way to recycle your old cards.

P

PARTIES

Parties needn't break the bank; ask each of your guests to bring a bottle and a dish of food to share – then all you have to do is organise the event.

PETROL – see Cars

POSTAGE

Use 2nd class whenever possible, or email if you can instead. Become familiar with the tariff for postage, according to size, and use the smallest possible envelope or package.

PRICE COMPARISON WEBSITES – see also Which?

These can be a convenient place to start when looking for the best price for goods or services. But beware, they are not all independent, and may only include companies who will benefit if they get customers through the site.

A price comparison website may not necessarily provide the cheapest quote; quotes can vary by hundreds of pounds. If you intend to use a price comparison website to find the best deal, be sure to check out more than one before making a decision. **http://paler.com/price_comparison** lists all the price comparison sites.
www.moneysupermarket.com

PRINTERS AND PRINTER INKS

If you are buying a printer, check the price of the inks which your preferred model uses, as ink prices vary enormously and affect the running cost.

Branded cartridges are a good deal more expensive than compatible inks, but be aware that you may be invalidating the warranty on your printer by using non-branded ink.
www.printerinks.com

REPAIRS

Do it yourself

Keeping things in good repair will help them last longer and save you having to buy a new one. If something in your home needs fixing, can you do it yourself?

Caution: electrical DIY can be dangerous and should be done by a qualified professional.

Learn the basics of household maintenance

There are a number of websites offering advice and instruction on anything from damp problems to fixing a leaking tap, and there are loads of books on household maintenance – try your local library.

Larger projects

For larger projects, e.g. building shelves, there may be evening classes in your area – check on your council's website, in your local newspaper or on your library notice board.

www.diyfixit.co.uk
www.ultimatehandyman.co.uk

Swap skills

Can you trade a skill for repair work – have you got a Local Exchange Trading Scheme (LETS) in your area?

www.letslinkuk.org for information on LETS and finding a local group.

SAVINGS

Save regularly

Save a little each week until you have enough to buy what you want, rather than using a credit card or overdraft and paying interest. Online savings accounts usually offer the best rates for regular savers. Why not open an easy-access savings account for different purposes, for example Christmas, car expenditure, holidays or telephone bills? Saving on a regular basis makes the arrival of bills less painful.

Get the best interest rate

If you have any savings, make sure they are in accounts which bring you the best rate of interest; the rates may well have changed since you opened the account. Be prepared to spend time moving your savings if necessary to follow the best interest rate.

Introductory offers
Beware of introductory offers on accounts and keep an eye on their end date.

Spread your savings
Under current legislation the Financial Services Compensation Scheme guarantees £50,000 of savings per person per institution – if you have savings, spread them across different institutions, remembering to allow for interest pushing the amount above the limit. Make sure that you do not put more than your guaranteed allowance into any one institution – some institutions include several different organisations which, unless they are registered with the FSA separately, means that you may unwittingly exceed your £50,000 limit.
www.moneysavingexpert.com for more detailed information.

Save over a set period
If you can put your money away for longer periods you will get a better rate of interest.

Use your tax-free allowance
Take advantage of tax-free savings through an ISA if you can, but again keep an eye on the rates as the months go by.

S

SELL YOUR SURPLUS STUFF – MAKE MONEY

Do you need everything in your home – can you stretch your cash by selling some of the things you no longer use? Have a good clear out – sell off your old CDs, books or goods at car boot sales or through online shops e.g. Amazon, eBay.

www.amazon.co.uk

www.ebay.co.uk

www.preloved.co.uk

www.gumtree.com a classified ads and community website which includes swaps.

www.U-exchange.com for swapping anything for free from houses to accountancy services.

SHOPPING – see also Electrical Appliances and Electronic Gadgets, Food, Travel

- Share your shopping trips with a friend and save money on petrol.

- Try and confine your 'big shop' to once a month.

- Use the pound shops and cheap outlets, e.g. cash and carry, for basics.

- Find out which shops have OAP discount days, and when they are – you can often get 10% off if you are eligible.

- Don't be afraid to offer to pay cash for a discount – you save the retailer money if you don't use plastic.

- Loyalty cards can save you money but avoid store cards, many of which charge hefty interest rates if you don't pay on time.

SPORT – see Leisure

STAMPS – See Postage

SUPERMARKETS – see Food

TELEPHONE

The prices and options for telephone calls, mobile and landline, are changing all the time as new services and deals come along. If you have the time and energy you can save a lot by keeping a close eye on charges and moving your account to suit; but beware of the small print and the extras which may not immediately be obvious when you are looking for a provider.

You can buy your telephone, broadband and television from one company in a bundled deal, but it can be cheaper, if more complicated, to buy line rental, local calls, international calls, calls to mobiles, and mobile phone calls separately (see below for websites to help you find the best deals). Since not all the price comparison websites are impartial, go to individual company websites to check actual costs. In all cases you need to check the small print and find out if you will be locked into a contract which you can't get out of easily or without penalty, before you commit to the service.

Landlines

There are two costs with using a landline – the rental and the calls, and the call cost depends on the type of number you are dialing. With a lot of persistence you can find the cheapest provider of both your line rental and the different types of call.

Revenue sharing numbers

0800 numbers are free from landlines, but avoid 0870 and 0845 numbers – you are paying hugely over the odds for the call and the company (including some councils!) you are calling is making money from your call; also avoid premium rate calls (starting with 09), favoured by TV phone-ins, which are even more expensive.

www.saynoto0870.co.uk gives alternative numbers you can use to avoid paying the high charges of 0870.
http://callchecker.moneysavingexpert.com to check latest prices of the different types of number.

Work out what type of call you make most from your landline, and then find the best deal. If you make a lot of international calls or mobile phone calls from a landline, investigate the tariffs of override providers.

Override providers

You can save a lot, especially if you have to call overseas, or a revenue sharing number, if you use an override provider, where you dial a prefix before the number and get a cheaper rate.
www.18185.co.uk
www.cheapestcalls.co.uk

Mobile phones

If you only use your mobile occasionally then pay as you go is your cheapest option, and with this system you cannot unknowingly overspend.

If you are a heavy user then a contract is worth checking out, but be sure to read the small print.

It is usually cheaper to send a text. If possible get on to the same network as your close friends and family and save money.

Bundled deals

Bundled deals can be a much cheaper way of doing things but check the small print on contracts with bundled services – will you be tied in for a long time? Does the service give you exactly what you want? Is there a connection fee? Do they charge for technical support? What services do you need to take to get 'free' broadband? What is included in 'free' calls and, even more important, what is not? Some providers include line rental in their packages – be aware that if you sign up to these and want to go back to renting your line from BT you may have to pay for reconnection.

If you can, make your calls at the cheapest time of day or week to make the most of any free calls in your package.
www.simplifydigital.com for the best bundled deals.

Internet telephony (making calls using your computer)
If you have a computer check out Skype (one of several pro-viders of Voice-over Internet Protocol, which is a telephone service available on the web). You can talk to anyone who also has Skype and it's free – great if you are calling friends and family who are abroad.
www.skype.com for free phone calls to other Skype users using your broadband connection.

TOILETRIES – see also Cosmetics
When you buy shampoo, soap or bubble bath you are paying a lot for the packaging and for the brand name. In some cases there are cheaper alternatives; for example witch hazel is a natu-ral astringent and toner, and Epsom salts can be used instead of bath salts. Both are available from chemists.

If you really want to save money, and you have the time and inclination, you can make your own toiletries for hair, face and body; there are a number of books and even courses on DIY beauty, it's fun to do and satisfying to know what has gone into the stuff you use on your skin.

www.allecogreenandbeautiful.co.uk and **www.starkhechara.co.uk** have recipes for making your own toiletries.

www.nealsyardremedies.com ☎ 0845 262 3145 for natural ingredients.

Caution: if you are making your own potions and are pregnant or breast feeding, check out the safety of any ingredients with your midwife or health visitor.

TOYS – see also Babies

Children, especially the under 5s, can have hours of fun with very simple household things, e.g. cardboard boxes, pots and pans and wooden spoons, and they cost next to nothing.

New toys, especially the larger ones, are costly and their lifespan is often short. You can save money by buying good-quality second-hand toys either online or through the local newspaper, or locally from car boot sales, charity shops or auctions. Be sure to check out the quality and condition of the toy you are buying for safety.

T

Try to avoid buying the latest craze toys – as soon as the craze is past the toy gets neglected; it can pay to get toys with a longer life which might cost a bit more up front – climbing frames, swings or slides, for example.

If your local library has a toy library you have access to a variety of toys which can be returned once the novelty has worn off; if there isn't one in your neighbourhood, why not start one? Or get together with friends and hold a toy swap party (without the children!).

www.natll.org.uk The National Association of Toy and Leisure Libraries is a charity offering information on how to start a toy library.
www.babycentre.co.uk for advice on buying second-hand toys.

TRAINS – see Travel

TRAVEL – see also Cars, Holidays
There are lots of little things you can do to save money when you need to go anywhere, from booking seats early for longer journeys, to planning ahead to reduce the number of local journeys you need to take.

Is hitchhiking for you? Hitchhiking Buddies matches people wanting rides with people driving in Europe.
www.hitchhikers.org

Buses

Get a travel pass

Check out any deals and travel passes; if you are over 60 you can travel free on buses all over the country – ask your local council for further information. Bus passes are free and, although there are a few rules to comply with, it is a wonderful facility to have. **www.direct.gov.uk** for information on free bus travel and concessions.

Get a season ticket

Get a season ticket if you travel a regular journey every day, or a day ticket or travel card if you do several journeys on one day.

Free buses

Take advantage of any free buses to your local shopping centre or, if you know what you want, save yourself a journey altogether by ordering online and having your goods delivered.

Get off the bus early

Can you save money by getting off a stop or two earlier and walking the rest of the way?

Find the cheap deals

If you are travelling further afield you can get to most parts of the UK for as low as £1 using Megabus if you book in advance. **www.megabus.com/uk**

www.nationalexpresseastcoast.com for deals from National Express.

Trains

Save booking fees

Booking online is easy but choose a site that does not charge a booking fee. If you book at your local station it's free. Remember to check to see whether it is cheaper to buy two singles rather than a return, or to split your train journey.

Book ahead

If you are travelling a long distance, booking in advance will save you money – advance tickets are the cheapest and are on sale 12 weeks ahead of your journey.

To get advance notice of any travel deals, sign up to newsletters or ticket alerts for information on when cheaper tickets are on sale.

www.ticketalert.thetrainline.com Train ticket website where you can sign up to get a ticket alert when advance tickets come on sale.

Get a season ticket

If you travel the same journey on a regular basis, it is almost always cheaper to get a season ticket.

http://ojp.nationalrail.co.uk/en/pj/sts to calculate your season ticket cost.

Get a railcard

Get a railcard if you are eligible – you will probably get the cost of the card back with the first journey you make.

www.railcard.co.uk gives details of railcards available.

Travel off-peak

Travel outside peak times on long journeys if you can – fares are cheaper.

www.thetrainline.com enables you to plan the cheapest time and day to travel in the UK.

Get an Oyster card

If you are travelling in London on public transport get an Oyster card from a London station or online and save money.

www.tfl.gov.uk/tickets to get an Oyster card online.

Find the cheap deals

www.megatrain.com the train section of the Megabus website.
www.seat61.com shows you how to go almost anywhere by train and has details of foreign train operators and how to plan your journey the cheapest way.

VOLUNTEERING

Why not volunteer some time, make new friends and get the satisfaction of doing something for someone else? Charity shops, local schools, conservation organisations, care homes, animal sanctuaries, hospitals and many other organisations all need people to help out.

Share your dog

Some care homes welcome well-behaved dogs as 'pat dogs'.
www.petsastherapy.org ☎ **01844 345 445**

Conservation

The British Conservation Trust offers opportunities for volunteers to help improve their local environment by doing anything from tree planting to creating wildlife habitats.
www2.btcv.org.uk ☎ **01302 388 883**

Earthwatch is an international environmental charity which provides opportunities for conservation volunteers on research teams.
www.earthwatch.org ☎ **01865 318 838**

The National Trust welcomes volunteers, from gardeners to room stewards.
www.nationaltrust.org.uk ☎ 01793 817632

Be a star
Help out with your local hospital radio.

Be a steward
Volunteer as a steward at one of the UK's music festivals and get to see some of the bands for free; Oxfam also has opportunities at festivals.
www.oxfam.org.uk ☎ 0300 200 1300

Be a farmer
Work on an organic farm – give some time in exchange for your bed and board and learn new skills at the same time – it costs £20 to join World Wide Opportunities on Organic Farms.
www.WWOOF.org.uk

Work abroad
Voluntary Service Overseas provides your fares, insurance, bed and board and a small allowance in exchange for you giving your time and skills to a community.
www.vso.org.uk ☎ 0208 780 7200

www.volunteering.org.uk ☎ **0845 305 6979** National Centre for Volunteering has a list of volunteer centres and lots of information on volunteering.

www.do-it.org.uk ☎ **0207 250 5700** is a registered charity providing a national database of volunteering opportunities.

WASHING AND DRYING CLOTHES

If you always make sure you have a full load and wash at a low temperature, or use the economy programme, you will save on your energy bills.

Try and avoid using a tumble dryer as they are very expensive to run; use an airer or washing line instead if you can.

Using half the amount of washing powder when your clothes are not very dirty, or even Eco balls, reduces the amount of detergent you buy. If you only have a few things to wash, why not wash by hand? Always ask yourself whether you can wear it one more time before it needs a wash.

WATER

- Depending on the number of people in your home, it is often cheaper to have a water meter. These can be installed free by your water company.

- If you have an old-style toilet, put a Hippo or 'Save a flush' device in it and save water – most water companies provide these for free.

- Unless yours is a power shower, having a shower rather than a bath saves a lot of water.

- Never leave a tap running, particularly when cleaning your teeth.

- Check regularly to make sure you have no leaks anywhere.

- Collect free rainwater from your roof in a water butt for your garden or for washing your car.

- Avoid using a sprinkler or a hose in the garden – they can use almost as much water in an hour as an average family of four uses in a day.

WEDDINGS

Your wedding need not cost you a fortune; there are loads of savings to be made by doing things yourself or getting friends and family to help.

Cake

Bake your own wedding cake, or, if there is a catering course at a local college, there may be a student who might like a project for the cost of the ingredients.

Catering

This can be a big expense; why not ask friends and relatives to help out – spread the load by asking a number of people to cook different dishes, and provide the ingredients.

Clothes

Your wedding clothes are usually only worn once, which is a lot of money for one day; check out charity shops, find a bargain in the sales, look for second-hand wedding outfits, or hire them.

DVD

If you want to record your big day, have you got a friend with a camcorder who will make you a DVD?

Flowers

If friends and relatives grow flowers in their gardens, can they help out with the flowers?

Honeymoon

Plan your honeymoon well in advance to take advantage of early booking discounts or, if you don't mind where you go, leave it until the very last minute and get a last-minute deal.

Photographs

Can you find a photography student who would be delighted to take your photos for a reduced fee?

Stationery

Wedding stationery needn't cost a lot; you can make your own by hand or, if you have one, use a computer to create invitations, order of service, menus and anything else you want printed, all with the same theme.

W

Transport

Have you got a friend with a posh car, a boat or a horse and cart who would be happy to get you to the wedding on time?

Venue

Why hire an expensive venue for your reception? Your local community centre or village hall will be much cheaper.
www.cheap-wedding-success.co.uk

WHICH?

One of the only websites offering unbiased advice on anything from gas suppliers to toasters. You can get 30 days' trial of Which? for £1 to find the best value for money; don't forget to cancel before the 30 days is up.
www.which.co.uk ☎ 01992 822800

WILLS

Making a will using a solicitor can be very expensive; if your will is straightforward you can do it yourself using a DIY form from a stationers or the web.
www.free-wills.co.uk

RESOURCES

WEBSITES
www.moneysavingexpert.com
www.gocompare.com
www.moneysupermarket.com
www.moneymagpie.com
www.thisismoney.co.uk
www.fool.co.uk
www.discount-age.co.uk Valerie Singleton's initiative to find deals for the over-60s.
www.5pm.co.uk and
www.toptable.co.uk to find good deals when booking restaurants.

BOOKS

Other Green Books Guides:

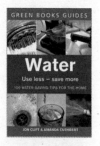

Water: use less – save more
by Jon Clift and Amanda Cuthbert
100 water-saving tips for the home.
£4.95 paperback

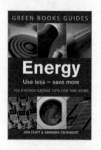

Energy: use less – save more
by Jon Clift and Amanda Cuthbert
100 energy-saving tips for the home.
£4.95 paperback

Reduce, Reuse, Recycle:
an easy household guide
by Nicky Scott
An A–Z guide to recycling.
£4.95 paperback

Cutting Your Car Use
by Anna Semlyen
Ideas for leaving the car at home.
£4.95 paperback

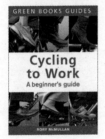

Cycling to Work: a beginner's guide
by Rory McMullan
Gives support and encouragement to get
to work by bike.
£4.95 paperback

**Eat Well, Waste Less: an A–Z guide
to using up leftovers**
by Bish Muir
Shows you how to use up your leftover food
to make delicious meals and save money.
£4.95 paperback